Jean S. Platt

Ribbons

By Jean S. Platt

PERSONA PRESS

PITTSBURGH, PENNSYLVANIA

1992

Cover Photography:
Gail N. Platt

Book & Cover Design:
Valenta Platt Design Group, Pittsburgh, PA

First Printing: November, 1992
Copyright © 1992, by Jean S. Platt
All rights reserved.
Printed in the U.S.A.
Library of Congress Catalog Card Number: 92-91043

Published in the United States by
PERSONA PRESS • 1004 Devonshire Road • Pittsburgh, PA • 15213

ISBN: 09634688-0-4

For My Husband

Illustrations

Childhood

"Titus" (Rembrandt's Son 1641-1668)
Rembrandt Harmenz Van Rign, Dutch, 1606-1669

Love & Marriage

"Ruben's Master & Wife"
Peter Paul Rubens, Flemish, 1577-1640

Celebration

"Singing Flute Player"
Franz Hals, Flemish, 1580-1668

Reflection

"Jan Cornelisz Sylvius, Preacher" Etching
Rembrandt Harmenz Van Rign, Dutch, 1606-1669

Contents

Preface

I. CHILDHOOD

II. LOVE AND MARRIAGE

Preface

As a mother of six, grandmother of nine, and great-grandmother of two, it occurs to me that by now I should have learned a little something about what really matters in life. What I have learned is this: our lives are like ribbons — ribbons that unite husband and wife, children, grandchildren, cousins, aunts and uncles — family; ribbons that reach out to friends and neighbors, associates, acquaintances, paperboys, milkmen, mailmen, supermarket clerks, doctors and nurses — a tangled mass of ribbons linking the generations, the races, the rich, the poor, the young, the old, the sick, the well, and those of diverse religious beliefs. I have learned that old cliches are to be believed: I am my brother's keeper, and the only real happiness in life comes from caring for — and about — those with whom the ribbons of our lives become entwined, and ultimately, reaching out to that larger family to which we all belong — the human race.

Moreover, I have become increasingly aware with the passage of time that life with all its challenges and problems is still a magnificent adventure and is meant to be lived with courage, conviction and joy!

RIBBONS

I

Childhood

First Birthday

He can hold
his own glass,
and he does
make a pass
at his mouth
with the spoon.
I believe
fairly soon
he'll be starting
to walk;
he's beginning
to talk.
He's made
splendid progress,
but in the
last summing,
I wish that
he understood
bathrooms and
plumbing.

New Mother

Carry her ever so gently;
careful, now, she mustn't fall.
Cover her well with her blanket;
it's chilly there in the hall.
Fetch her the bottle of warm milk;
there it is high on the shelf.
Maybe it's best if I help you;
you can't quite reach it yourself.

Place the wee bottle beside her;
push the crib close to the wall;
wise little two-year-old mother,
wonderful first baby doll.

Con Artist

My visitor is not quite three,
a challenge to my sanity:
he bugs me when I'm on the phone;
he helps himself to my cologne
(and smells divine); he slams the doors
and tracks mud in on all my floors.

His scribblings on the bedroom wall
and hieroglyphics (center hall)
don't say a lot artistically,
but there they are for all to see.
His cookie crumbs are everywhere—
the sofa, rug, and easy chair.

Exploding with vitality,
he's clever too; he knows that he
will be forgiven — all is bliss
when grandma gets a hug and kiss.

Milestone

"Look," said the smile, and the brown eyes danced.
I looked — I gaped — I stood entranced
at the dress on backwards and inside out,
the sweater needing a turnabout,
the right foot wearing the left foot's shoe,
and one yellow stocking, the other bright blue.
But the little face beamed with such self-pride
that the laughter rising within me died;
she had done this all by herself, you see;
she was "all dressed up" with no help from me.

"Look," said the smile, and the brown eyes shone.
I looked and saw of a sudden she'd grown,
and I knew as I gathered and held her tight
that our children grow out of our arms overnight.

Panacea

The morning started badly;
he went off without his hat,
and worse — he didn't wear his boots;
he knows my views on that.
And after school he handed me—
he's only in first grade!—
a "treatise" from his teacher
on his latest escapade.
Then, banished to his bedroom
to reflect upon the day,
he was distressed, and so was I
when friends arrived to play.
But later, when I went upstairs
to start a dialogue,
I found him sleeping: at his side—
his old, beloved dog.

Mother's Day

He teases his sister
and torments the cat;
he can't find his mittens
and won't wear his hat;
the daily epistles
from nursery school
convince me his teacher
is losing her cool.
And yet he remembered;
he gathered today—
bright, golden dandelions
for a bouquet.

First Love

Alas, it is true; I can see in his face
that his nursery school teacher has taken my place.
I knew it today when he went off to school
with a bright yellow crocus. (I'm nobody's fool.)

I'll simply ignore it; I've learned in the past—
his brothers are older — these things never last.
Her reign will be brief; you can ask any mother;
like me, she will soon be replaced by another.

On Faith

The small boy on the tricycle
careening down the walk
and greeting all the passersby,
engaging them in talk—
how sure he is of finding welcome
everywhere he goes,
of strangers wanting to be friends,
and yet, what small boy knows
the longing for companionship
within the lonely heart?
He will in time, but now, it seems
he simply must impart
the joy that fills his spirit
on this morning, just unfurled,
to all he meets within the bounds
of his delightful world:
how absolute, the confidence
inherent in a child;
how consummate, the faith—
without exception; undefiled.

Tomboy

She enters — a vision in pretty pastels;
her hair is beribboned; my foolish heart swells
when she puts her face up next to mine for a kiss:
was ever a granddaughter lovely as this?

Her pinafore's starched, and it stands stiffly out
as she prances and pirouettes; whirling about,
she moves with astonishing presence and grace—
this four-year-old charmer in velvet and lace.

A playmate arrives, and with wings on their feet
they race to the playground; it's just down the street.
She's back in a while, and my eyes open wide
when I open the door and she scampers inside.

Her ribbons are gone, and her hair is a mess;
Her shoes are untied; there's a rip in her dress;
her knee has a scrape; there's a smudge on her face
and grass stain all over the velvet and lace.

Oh, how could I let myself be so deceived?
And where is the image that I had conceived?—
demure little girl? — devotee of the dance?
What nonsense! This child needs a sweatshirt and pants.

Femme Fatale

The pendulum earrings that swing from her ears,
the make-up that startles the eye,
the golden hair swept to the top of her head,
the spike heels — all tend to belie
the person I know to be dwelling inside
that brazen, misleading veneer;
confusing, indeed, I will have to admit,
but, in truth, what would seem to appear
part angel, part devil, part lady, part tramp—
a curious, improbable mix—
is not so disturbing if one can recall
the foibles of females at six.

The Tree House

The yard's alive with little boys
(construction workers — lots of noise).
They've come with hammer, saw, and nails,
a length of rope and several pails
of paint; we have a maple tree
that suits their project perfectly.

At fever pitch they saw away
and paint and hammer till one day
of endless silence; then I know
they've finished it — a place to go
to tell their tales and dream their dreams:
in retrospect it almost seems
just yesterday a maple tree
provided such a place for me.

Granddaughter

Old faded blue jeans trimmed in beads,
long shining hair, a face that needs
no make-up — she is just thirteen.
Her older sister, seventeen,
has several beaus and she has none;
she'd settle happily for one.

She scarcely can await the day
one calls on her. I'd like to say,
"Be patient, child; your time will come,"
but I remember there were some
who told me that. (As I recall,
I needed no advice at all).

Thirteen — expectant, anxious age;
the adolescent views the stage
and eagerly awaits a part.
I sense the longing in her heart,
for somewhere in my memory
her counterpart lies buried: me.

Last Day of School

Exploding through the corridors,
they tumble down the stairs
and spill out over tree-lined walks
and busy thoroughfares.
And in the air, a simple chant
familiar to my ears
has struck a strong, responsive chord
and stripped away the years.
"No more classes, no more books,"
I hear the children shout,
and I'm a child again in June—
the day that school lets out.

Choirboy

"Sing praises unto Him, rejoice":
How sweetly the soprano voice
beseeches us; eyes fixed ahead,
he passes with slow, measured tread
in solemn and reflective mien—
a Botticelli figurine.

What exaltation on his face;
what innocence, what perfect grace,
and yet I cannot reconcile
this cherub coming down the aisle
with images I hold; is he
the one whose room appears to be
an annex to the local zoo?
This "paragon," if you but knew,
shares quarters with a guinea pig,
a hamster in a whirligig,
a snake, a rabbit, and three fish;
and, oh, how fervently I wish
that he — just once — would acquiesce
to cleaning up the awful mess.

How thoroughly this fetching child
has captivated and beguiled
the congregation (all but me);
I see his somewhat differently:
this lamb who fills their heart with joy —
outside these portals, he's all boy.

Viewpoint

The hour's late and I've been waiting up,
and he can't comprehend why I'm upset;
he's seventeen and thinks himself a man;
I'd like to cite the differences, and yet
I once was seventeen and understand
his inability to grasp the measure of
devotion, dedication, and concern
implicit in the term "parental love."

The generation gap is hard to bridge,
and yet I know when time replays this scene
with him performing in the parent role,
he'll understand my view of seventeen.

Summer's End

The summer's slipping fast away;
each day seems shorter now,
and curfew must be redefined;
a mother must allow
some recompense for summer's end;
remember what a lark—
to play the favorite childhood games
when it was growing dark?

I hear the children's laughter
and know their ecstasy:
at one with them at summer's end,
the child who lives in me.

II

Love and Marriage

A Valentine from My Love

What joy, my love, the postman brought
along with him today;
how wonderful, the things you do
in your old-fashioned way:
this frilly heart imploring me
to be your valentine—
did you not know the day we met
I staked you out as mine?

Reflections of a Honeymoon

In Tenerife, geraniums on terra cotta floors,
and in Madrid, old photographs of handsome toreadors,
a vista from Valencia of lemon trees in bloom,
the armoire in Segovia that dwarfed the tiny room;
Toledo, and El Greco prints on walls of pristine white,
and Malaga — the view at dusk of harbor ships alight:
how disparate, the lodgings to which we held a key,
yet each — when shared with you, my love—
was hearth and home to me.

Page From a Bride's Diary

My conversation, recently,
reveals a shift from "I" to "we":
"I (we) think this" — "I (we) feel thus;"
when one's in love, it's "we" and "us."

I note a lesser use of "my,"
and more of "our;" to simplify:
"my" dreams have now become "our" dreams
(he's really part of me, it seems).

We're taught that one and one are two
and none can argue that it's true;
with lovers, though, this comes undone,
for two in love can be as one.

Patterns

Of all the fathers I recall,
mine had to be the best of all.
I loved to feel his hands on mine
when we washed up at supper time,
and later, when we went upstairs,
I wanted him to hear my prayers.
He was the one to dim the light
when I had said my last good-night.

And mother — being special too—
quite understood my point of view.
She knew that time brings changes and
would, one day, disengage my hand
from his, so I could then be free
to search for someone just for me.
My choice (I know it made her glad)
turned out to be a lot like Dad.

Bride's Lament

How proudly I served him his favorite dishes,
expecting he'd tell me that they were delicious.
I followed her recipes. (Could there be others?)
He found them "quite good," though "not just like" his mother's,
and thinking that never again would I bother,
I wondered — had she heard the same from his father?

For My Valentine

This fellow in the skivvy shirt
indulging in a nap,
his glasses slipping down his nose,
the paper in his lap,
this fellow with the little paunch
and secondary chin,
the hairline that's receding—
the crown that's wearing thin;
this once resplendent, gallant knight
(in obvious decline)
is still the only one I'd choose
to be my valentine.

The Marriage Seesaw

Like children on a seesaw,
we've occasion to assess
both parts of the equation,
the balance of the stress:
a marriage has uneven times
(we've been through high and low);
aware, we promised when we wed—
how many years ago?—
the two of us would make it work,
each striving constantly
to bring it balance; oh, my love,
you do — eternally!

The Perceptive Heart

I hoped I'd chosen wisely when we wed;
I loved you, and you seemed so right for me,
but love impairs the vision, it is said;
with stardust in the eyes it's hard to see.

Now you are lover, confidant, and friend;
a father reminiscent of my own.
You've taught me to be firm, and–yes–to bend,
and, more important, how to stand alone.

My eyes are clear of stardust, now, and see
(my heart's conclusion many years ago)
no one but you could be so right for me;
I'm glad my heart perceived that it was so.

The Need I Have For You

Your humor in the morning
when the sky is overcast,
your patience in the evening
when I know that mine won't last.
That rumpus in the children's room—
the six o'clock melee—
will dissipate when you arrive
and in your easy way
unite the adversaries
and restore the peace again—
a gift that surely ranks you
with the noblest of men.
I've no desire for worldly things
my wants, it seems, are few,
but, oh, my love, how infinite,
the need I have for you.

Forgiving: A Poem For My Husband

I gazed upon you sleeping like a child,
and when you woke to find me there, you smiled
and drew me close. I was remorseful, then,
remembering that hurtful moment when
my tongue betrayed me, lending voice to thought
which, even then, I knew was best forgot.
But, you, my love, possessed of special grace,
a gift with which you pardon and efface
imprudent words — how freely you forgive
and by example teach me how to live.

Reflections on a Winter Night

The winter wind is wild tonight;
maniacally it lashes out,
and attic shutters, loosened now,
are caught up in the fury of the storm.
In cadence — like a metronome—
they crash against the siding of the house.

Inside, the old house creaks and groans,
and windows, rattling fearfully,
exact a sort of eerie counterpoint.
The ghost up in the transom moans,
aroused and agitated by the wind.

You settle in your easy chair
with book and apple close at hand;
your quiet strength a citadel
against my mindless terror of the night.
I put a favorite record on,
and when your eyes meet mine, my love,
they reaffirm the joy of man and wife.

On Being a Mother

Is there a one who doesn't know
(when parenting has hit a low)
the longing now and then to be
a child again at Father's knee?
And is there one who doesn't feel
(when schisms take too long to heal)
the yearning, once again, to rest
secure against a mother's breast?

Ah, adolescence; that's a stage
of inner turmoil, outer rage:
I'd quite forgotten until now
that, then, a mother must allow
(for callow youth's time-honored fling)
some loosening of the apron string.
What tribulation, omnipresent,
coping with the adolescent!

Now from the vaults of memory
come images reminding me
of difficult, confusing years
and Father's tirades, Mother's tears.
How infinite, the trials inherent
in the role of caring parent,
and, at times, I long to be
a child again at Father's knee.

Rediscovery

Remember, love, the ecstasy
of bride and groom — just you and me.
Soon we were three, and shortly, four;
the years slipped by, and we were more.
We stopped the count at three plus three
(three boys for you, three girls for me).
Our house was filled with all the noise
that comes with raising girls and boys:
the telephone, the radio,
strange music on the stereo.
No longer merely man and wife,
we were immersed in family life.

What happy times to look back on
with all the children grown and gone,
and yet, my love, what ecstasy—
to be, again, just you and me.

Question:
What's it Like to Rear a Large Family?

Say it's been lovely — or hectic — whatever;
say there was never a lull;
tell them that somehow you managed to weather it;
say that it never was dull.

Say it was difficult; say it was great;
say that you're glad you're alive;
say it's important to choose the right mate —
essential if one would survive.

Say it's delightful — that time goes too fast,
and tell of the good times you knew;
but add that the youngest got married — at last! —
and it's lovely, again, to be two.

Flashback

I stood outside the jewelry store today
while waiting for my ever tardy bus,
and as I viewed the wedding ring display,
my thoughts were of another June and us,
remembering the day long years ago
when we selected rings, and my heart knew
there was no need to look at jewels to know
in all the world none could compare to you.
How vividly the scene came back to me—
the two of us together in the store,
my heart, so full that I could not foresee
a time to come when I would love you more.
The years have passed; together we've grown old,
and you are still my choice "to have and hold".

A Grandmother's Tenet For The Bride

Tomorrow is your wedding day;
reflections fill my mind
as I recall the old cliche
which warns that love is blind,
but you have chosen wisely, dear
(as far as I can tell);
your groom-to-be, it would appear,
can have no parallel.
I wish you all the happiness
that marriage would intend,
but my first wish, I must confess,
is love that knows no end.
And what I want with all my heart
on this, your wedding eve,
is your regard while I impart
a tenet I believe:
to give your marriage special grace
and help it to transcend
the problems it may have to face,
be not just wife, but friend.
A grandmother, I know, thereof,
how blessed is the life
where friendship grows along with love
between a man and wife.

Time-Honored Lovers

I saw them on a bench inside the park,
their white heads close, and I won't soon forget
her fingers resting on his gnarled hand:
time-honored lovers…I can see them yet.

And then I saw the boy and girl in jeans—
not twenty yet, but clearly, lovers too,
and I recalled those incandescent days
when you and I were young, and love was new.

How disparate, the lovers in this world,
yet all of them akin to you and me:
time-honored lovers holding hands at dusk—
what hopes, my love, within that memory.

For My Love

For hours, reading quietly beside the fire,
we two have been content, no cause to speak
when, suddenly (you didn't say what prompted it),
you rose and came to kiss me on the cheek.
In 40 years of marriage there were happenings—
the birth of sons and daughters through the years,
and birthday parties, graduations — happy times
that, somehow, one remembers more than tears.
How strange, that in a myriad of memories
(if you should be the first, my love, to go)
this moment — when you came to kiss me on the cheek —
will be among the treasured ones, I know.

Seasons of a Happy Marriage

While cleaning out the attic when we moved,
I came across a carton filled with toys
and, suddenly, envisioned them again
in those complaisant days, our girls and boys.

And when your hand reached out to gather mine,
I knew that you were wandering through the years
along with me; I saw the other hand
reach up to wipe at unexpected tears.

Through summer much too soon has followed spring,
the mind will treasure highlights for recall;
and you and I will wander country lanes
and revel in the dividends of fall.

Testimony of Love

I wear the mantle of your love
whenever you're away,
wrapped tightly when the winds are fierce—
and in the month of May,
draped lightly on my shoulders,
and yet I feel it there,
reminding me I'm not alone
but half, still, of a pair.

I wear the mantle of your love
because my foolish heart—
we're married nearly fifty years!—
still grieves when we're apart.

Transition

When they were small, our girls and boys,
the old pine chest held lots of toys:
a fuzzy rabbit, beads on strings,
a teddy bear, all sorts of things—
a monkey and a one-armed doll
were in that toy chest in the hall.
On rainy days, I must attest,
no ransom could have bought that chest.
Then came the years of radio,
"their" music on the stereo,
a washer constantly awhirl
with jeans for every boy and girl,
and anything not deemed germane
to adolescence, it was plain,
was worthless — it had seen its day,
so toys and box were put away.
Those full complaisant years moved on;
the children, all grown-up, are gone,
but now the thought occurs to me
it might be provident to see
if any toys are still about;
it's time to get the toy box out.
What energy! What fun! What noise!
the grandchildren: bring on the toys!

The Old Couple

Whenever he would tell her
that he was of a mind
to take a stroll around the town
she wouldn't stay behind
for any household chore — her hand in his,
they wandered through the square;
sometimes they picnicked in the park;
I often saw them there.
He slipped away from her one night,
and (as I knew she would)
she rose to custom's harsh demands—
did all the things she should
and did them well: she took each proffered hand
and smiled and made small talk,
and for the final services
put on his favorite frock.
She sat erect until the end;
then, standing in the aisle,
requested to be taken home alone to rest a while.
But after she had gone inside
and hung her coat and hat,
and sat a moment in his chair
to stroke the little cat,
she looked out toward the garden—
she had heard a voice — and then,
with wildly beating heart she rose
and followed him again.

Eulogy For a Son

The two white heads were bowed and almost touching;
his gnarled fingers curled around her hand
and they were silent — lost in reminiscence,
the past encroaching on the present now.

A lifelong friend arose to read the scripture:
time honored words of comfort for their grief;
They raised their heads and fixed their eyes upon him,
their faces in repose; there were no tears

The service ended, and they sat unmoving,
until at last, he turned to look at her.
Her eyes, which had been dull with pain and sorrow,
were filled with tears; the healing had begun.

Reprieve

The old man sat in silence, but his thumbs
betrayed his anguish, circling endlessly,
and every nervous clearing of his throat
touched off a little cycle of response:
He raised his coat sleeve, scrutinized his watch,
then set his thumbs to spinning round again.
We furtively observed his every move,
not one of us believed she would survive,
and he was dreaming — wandering through the years;
they'd been together almost sixty-five.
A nurse appeared and all eyes questioned her;
her manner had been brusque the day before
until she learned what we already knew;
then her compassion could not be denied.
Her softened presence added credence to
the dark suspicion growing in our minds.
But now this woman told us with a smile
(what joy it must evoke in one to give
the unexpected news of a reprieve)
the surgery was over; she would live.
The old man knew that this reprieve was brief,
but all that mattered now was that she lived;
his tongue released a rush of dammed up words
which flowed unchecked—there seemed to be no end
until the nurses wheeled her in the room;
then he fell silent once again and wept.

Widow's Legacy

How glorious the morning was
when you were here with me;
how wonderful to greet the day
and share the ecstasy
of robin's reveille at dawn
and mourning dove's lament,
the swiftly fading crescent moon,
the sun in its ascent;
the pearl of dew upon a rose
just starting to unfold,
the honeysuckle's sweet bouquet,
the pungent marigold.

What joy it is to find, my love,
ascending now in me,
your all-embracing love of life,
a blessed legacy.

Images : The Widow's Treasury

The heart must choose which images to keep,
and these, selected for their special glow,
are some of mine — the best, by far, of all,
though not preserved in film portfolio:
those quiet winter evenings by the fire,
you with a book and me with pen in hand,
the midnight walks along a moonlit beach,
our footprints close together in the sand;
the picnics when the black-eyed Susans bloomed
upon the meadow where we two would lie
delineating figures in the clouds
that billowed overhead in summer's sky.
The heart must choose which images to keep—
to treasure in the vaults of memory,
and these, selected by my prudent heart,
will comfort me until eternity.

New Widow

"My husband; this was on our wedding day;
how thin he was." I hadn't meant to stay;
a neighbor, I had merely come to call
and ask if I could take her to the mall.
But there were things she wanted me to see,
and so, together on the old settee,
we looked at snapshots of a way of life
where she had reveled in the role of wife:
the children she was proud of — girl and boy,
the grandchildren, her special pride and joy.
The past was all, for she could not allow
the future to intrude upon her now.
And yet I knew her faith would light the way,
and strengthen her a little every day
until that undetermined moment when,
triumphantly, she would move on again.

Tradition

We gathered often at their house
for fun and family fare,
and grandpa always offered grace,
a very special prayer.

We came together recently—
the first since he was gone,
his absence weighing heavily,
and yet we carried on:

At supper time we gathered round,
each wondering anxiously
if there was one to take his place,
unable to foresee
that grandma was the chosen one;
she sat, now, in his chair—
her faith a challenge to us all—
and offered grandpa's prayer.

III

Celebration

Carousel

Remember that ride on the carousel—
your first — and the endless wait
till the man came around and released the chain
that held you at the gate?
Remember, at last, astride the mount,
what rapture filled your soul
as the prancing steed went round and round
and up and down the pole?
And the lights were bright and the music, sweet,
and when you reached the top,
you could see balloons and the crowds below
and wished it would never stop?

Oh, life is a glorious carousel,
and there's nothing to portend
(when the lights are bright and the music sweet)
that the ride will ever end.
So choose your charger, command him well,
observe; there is much to see.
What joy to be here on the carousel;
"Hosanna!" from you and from me.

April

If asked to describe her, I guess I would say
less restless than March, less placid than May
with robins appearing again on the sill
and yellow forsythia high on the hill.

If asked to describe her, I guess I would tell
of bright golden daffodils down by the dell,
of blossoms beginning to bloom on the trees
and heavenly fragrance adrift on the breeze;
of lambs in the meadow and foals in the glen—
a world, winter-weary, reviving again.

If asked to describe her, how could I impart
the wonder that April evokes in my heart?

Easter

When crocuses and daffodils
are blooming in the glen,
and lambs cavort, and all is lush and green,
my foolish heart accelerates,
delighted, once again,
that spring is here; how lovely, life's routine.
Oh, winter is a special time
with softly falling snow,
bright stocking caps, and Christmas season cheer;
with skaters and tobogganers
and cherry logs aglow,
but life begins anew when Easter's here.

A Prayer for Thanksgiving

For cherished moments of the past,
for pleasures of the present,
and when the path is dimly lit
for faith that's incandescent;
for dreamers who hold fast to dreams
to rise above despair,
for caring neighbors, loyal friends,
the healing power of prayer;
for all these blessings, large and small,
along life's passageway,
our special thanks, again, dear Lord,
on this Thanksgiving Day.

Christmas

Oh, Christmas is a magic time,
a cherished legacy,
the season of the innocent,
a splendid apogee
of adoration for the Child
who lived so long ago,
a time of selflessness and joy,
a time for all to know
the shades of night will rise upon
a glorious new day;
till then the star of Bethlehem
still shines to light the way.

Resurrection

Above, a sky that threatened
still another dismal day;
below, a soiled coverlet
that wouldn't melt away.
But then I saw the crocus
and my heart began to sing:
how glorious, the promise
of a reawakening!

The Innocents

Lord, bless the child who comes to offer help
instinctively, not having to be told,
the heart that offers kindness, unaware
that kindness is returned a hundredfold.

Among the countless treasures of my life,
the innocents, how beautiful and rare,
the child who, unadmonished, comes to help,
the loving heart that knows naught but to share.

For My Husband
(recovered after a long illness)

The lilac blooms outside the kitchen door,
and suddenly the tulips are ablaze;
bright sunshine spills across the old plank floor
(dust particles are dancing in the haze),
and skies are blue; spring sweeps across the land.
Her loveliness enthralls me, and my heart
leaps like a silly schoolgirl's when your hand
encircles mine; we've been so long apart.
The robin reappears, soft breezes blow,
and life is full — you're home again with me;
I cherish every moment now I know
how desolate without you life can be.
Near fifty years have passes since we were wed,
but, oh, my love — still sweet, the years ahead.

Anniversary Poem

As flaming colors are to fall
and robins to the spring,
the music to the carousel
and crowns to the king;
a baseball mitt to little boys,
a doll to little girls,
so you've become a part of me
as married life unfurls.
When memory evokes
the telling moment of my life,
I hear again the sacred vows
that made us man and wife.

The Vintage Years

How sweet I find the vintage years—
their late, abundant yield,
rewarding as the final harvest
gathered from the field:
the friendship that develops
from some latter-day pursuit,
the wonder and excitement
of a new and different route.
How colorful, the sunset
at the closing of the day;
how glorious with winter near,
the sweet, autumnal stay.
I add my voice to alleluiahs
offered by my peers
for these — perhaps the best of all—
the golden, vintage years.

Recapitulation

How spirited, this life; we move apace,
at times, beleaguered, yearning to efface
the burden or the problem we deplore
(the one we cannot, seemingly, ignore),
and yet, bestowed a multitude of ways,
how infinite, the blessings of our days.

Life offers challenge — moments of distress
and times of tribulation and duress,
but none can match the measure of delight
this wondrous gift continues to incite,
and when, from time to time, they're tallied up,
they transcend all, the blessings in my cup.

Friendship

How unpredictable is life—
the days of joy and sorrow,
the sweet tranquility, the strife,
the undefined tomorrow;
and what a joy, the special friend—
the one who's always there
to share the celebration,
or kneel with us in prayer.

The View From Here

When I was young, I thought the world
was spinning round for me;
I saw it as a proving ground,
myself, a nominee
for singular accomplishment—
what wild, ambitious schemes
are plausible when one is young
and filled with foolish dreams!

How glorious is youth, and yet,
what joy when one matures
to find (though dreams are unfulfilled)
that beauty still endures:
the sunrise, sunset, starry night—
incomparable display;
how wonderful, the view from here;
what blessings in each day!

The Flame of Hope

Like candles on a birthday cake
which flicker, burning low,
hope needs eternal vigilance
to keep the flame aglow;
yet, kept alive, it can sustain
the vigil in the night,
and, nurtured, will flare up again,
a beacon, burning bright.

The Loyal Friend

Her outlook and her smile belie her years;
she is herself, devoid of sham or pose;
her warmth consoles; her lively humor cheers;
she savors life, and yet how well she knows
its burdens can be difficult to bear.
She is a rock and can be counted on
when darkness covers all, and she has stayed
until the darkness yielded to the dawn,
and at those times the dawn has been delayed—
her love is constant — she has still been there:
life's gifts are legion, seeming without end,
and none more precious than a loyal friend.

Reminder

How constant are the challenges of life,
the quandaries, uncertainties, and strife;
no match for life's benevolence, and yet,
mere mortals, there are times when we forget.
Upon consideration one will find,
no matter what the problem on the mind,
with faith and hope — the strength that comes through prayer,
the burden never more than one can bear.

The Believers

One day the two came strolling through the park
and sat down on a bench across from me—
the old man and his grandson, just turned four,
delightful in their camaraderie.

The scene evoked an image from the past
of two extruded form the self-same mold:
one life, as destined, drawing to a close,
the other, just beginning to unfold.

And yet, how strong the bond that linked these two;
each welcomed morning as a trusted friend,
the herald of the day, and every day—
a promise to fulfill from start to end.

Sonnet For The Seasons

Spring likes pastels and will arrive, I know,
in palest pinks and yellows and chartreuse;
sometime in April (there may still be snow)
she will begin to don her lovely hues.
And summer,then, will follow close behind
in colors from a crayon box, bright and bold;
she wears them all; I don't believe you'll find
a one that she has chosen to withhold.
Fall has panache and will elect to wear
the brilliant reds and golds (her colors blaze);
enthralled, the world will gather round to stare;
her raiment never ceases to amaze.
And winter favors white year after year;
what blessings, these — the seasons of the year.

IV

Reflection

The Old Man

The old man (never married, I am told)
whose longish, snow-white hair could use a trim,
whose shirts and ties are constantly at odds,
whose coat is frayed and hangs too long on him,
whose jacket lacks a button on one sleeve,
whose trouser cuffs and pockets need repair,
whose sister died (the one who cared for him)—
how obvious that she's no longer there.
I've heard (but not from him, you can be sure)
the reasons that he never took a spouse;
he helped his widowed sister raise her sons
and bought the unpretentious little house
they shared for years, and when they went to school,
he paid the boys' tuition; now they're gone
(both working out of state), and he's alone,
a man near eighty left to carry on.
And yet, what humor in those twinkling eyes;
how he enjoys the little coterie
of loyal friends who gather every day
to share the pleasure of his company.
How constant is the dictate of his heart;
how passionate, his love of life; how rare—
each day, a gift to savor with his friends:
how blessed is the heart that needs to share.

Hidden Blessings

How frail our trust; how fragile our belief;
how frequently that happening construed
as tragedy becomes, in retrospect,
a blessing when examined and reviewed.
How rare the heart that ponders and perceives
what's hidden in the burden it receives.

Solitude

The soul needs quiet time for inspiration,
a lesson I have learned explicitly
from days that stretch to weeks with no allowance
for solitude — that special time for me
to weigh opinion, sort out truth and value,
and reaffirm again what I believe;
to think upon the choices I am making,
and mark, once more, the goals I would achieve.

The soul needs quiet time for self-communion,
assessment of priorities, and then—
with faith and hope renewed, the joy of living
will swell the heart to bursting once again.

Grandmother

Two small red-headed boys - one, five; one, eight-
are pounding on my door, arriving straight
from school. (I guess they might have changed their shoes;
the younger one's aren't tied.) How he amuses
me; those eyes of his that twinkle bright as stars
are looking past me now for candy bars.

I've cleared it with their mother — half my age
(who thinks I'm old enough to be a sage),
to give the boys a treat when they arrive.
They're here! Once more the house becomes alive
with laughter and exuberance and noise —
and I remember other little boys.

Seedlings

How can I tell my daughter
(who has sons and daughters in their teens,
creating problems, making scenes)
solutions are not quick or clear
when adult viewpoint counters peer.

How can I tell my daughter
(who is wondering what will happen next)
that there's no proven perfect text
for coping with the wayward young—
we would have heard its praises sung.

How can I tell my daughter
(who is disenchanted and confused),
"Dear, I'm not worried, just amused.
We managed to, by trial and error,
reclaim you—a holy terror!"

Granddaughter's Birthday

She stands before the bedroom mirror
trying her new dress;
her parents' eyes betray their thoughts
(mine, too, I must confess).
I understand their mixed emotions—
share their pride, and yet,
like them, I find it mingled with nostalgia and regret:
the little girl of yesterday
today turns seventeen;
oh, would that time could stay a while
those fleeting years between.

The Boy With The Bright Red Balloon

They came every day to the neighborhood park;
I waited for them to arrive;
she settled herself on a bench while the boy—
ecstatic at being alive—
raced to the playground and slid down the slide,
and then at the bottom, turned 'round
to do it all over again; how he laughed
as he slid on his seat to the ground.

I carried my camera over there once,
one memorable afternoon;
he posed for me, smiling and holding aloft
a wonderful, bright red balloon.

Years later I saw her again on the bench;
delighted, I asked for the boy,
and now I don't go to the park anymore
to relive those moments of joy:
The boy went away to a war he decried;
his laughter was over too soon;
no, I won't return to the park, nor will he—
the boy with the bright red balloon.

The Widow and The Check-Out Girl

Politics and candidates
and T.V. superstars,
the weather and inflation
and the price of candy bars:
how strong, the sense of unity
in all they talked about—
the widow and the single girl
who checked her groceries out.
And just as obvious, the bond
(though never quite declared)
that smiles and small talk couldn't hide—
the loneliness they shared.

Retrospection

What joy to find that patience comes with age
and mitigates the chafing at the wait—
the minutes and the hours and the days
preceding some anticipated date.

Youth hungers for tomorrow, unaware
how swift the journey through life's passageway:
tomorrow comes too soon for one to know
and savor all the wonder of today.

For a Friend

Now, when despair and tragedy
intrude upon your days,
and grief becomes a constancy
no course of action stays,
have faith; He sees your tribulation,
listens to your plea,
and He will soothe your anguished heart;
till then, come lean on me.

Eulogy For a Neighbor's Son

I thought the early morning mine
that day in June so long ago,
until I heard him call his dog;
then, seated on the patio,
I saw him dance across the yard,
the grass still wet with dew. What joy!—
to watch him, unobserved, and know
the ecstasy of one small boy.

His life, so brief, was not to have
an afternoon or evening; still —
he loved the morning so, he danced,
and, in my memory, always will.

Full Circle

The old man sleeps — an embryo —
knees drawn up to his chest,
I hesitate to waken him;
perhaps it might be best
to let him dream a little yet;
he looks so peaceful there,
and life is so confusing now,
the happy moments, rare.

But even as I stand and watch,
he wakes to gaze at me.
No recognition on his face,
he stares; then suddenly
he beckons with a fragile hand
to bring me to his side.
(He wants someone to comb his hair;
he hasn't lost his pride.)

I hold the mirror when I'm through;
he's pleased; his hair looks fine.
Three score — the years I've been his child;
now, for a while, he's mine.

The Recruiter

My four-year-old neighbor is here with his bat,
and it's obvious what's on his mind;
my grandchild, who hits pretty well — for a girl
(and, at times, is the best he can find).

But she isn't here now, so next on his list
is my son (and he's gone for the day);
undaunted, my caller suggests number three,
my husband — too weary to play.

The lower lip trembles; the blue eyes implore;
how fervent — how poignant — his plea;
so, off with the apron; the dishes can wait —
it seems that his last choice is me!

Observations of a Grandmother

I see the calm assurance in your eyes
and hear the firm conviction in your voice,
and I'm impressed. How can you be so wise—
so certain when you have to make a choice?
No matter what the question—you are there
with answers that are absolutely right;
I'm sure you must be happily aware
that you are very young to be so bright.
And yet—in reminiscing, I recall
a time when I was confident and sage.
Like you, I nearly always knew it all;
I was, perhaps, sixteen—about your age.

Grandpa's Rocking Chair

We had the rocker twenty years;
bought when the house was new,
it welcomed him right from the start;
it was "his" chair—he knew
that we had bought it just for him;
I still can see him there,
regaling all the grandchildren
assembled 'round the chair.
He'd play his old harmonica,
and dinner was delayed
till he'd run through his repertoire
and all requests were played.
As time ordained, we added props:
a pillow for the seat,
a stool (the doctor ordered it
to elevate his feet),
an afghan, soft as thistledown,
to cushion shoulder blades,
and still the old man played for us
his homespun serenades.
The chair is gone, and so is he,
our gallant troubadour,
but ever in my memory
I'll find him, as before,
contentedly ensconced within
his old beloved chair,
enchanting all the followers
who gather 'round him there.

On Kites and Dreams

A dream—like a kite with a glorious tail—
is a paradox, fragile, yet able to scale
unbelievable heights and (carefully tended)
soar, though, admittedly, hope is suspended
abruptly when either is dashed to the ground,
and fragments and tatters lie scattered around.
But hope is eternal, and one learns to mend:
the kite can be flown again; dreams need not end.

Guidelines for Grandma

I listened intently, I nodded, I smiled
at the long list of guidelines she left for the child—
his feeding, his playtime, his bath, and his nap—
explicit, allowing no chance for mishap.
And then she was gone and, ignoring the list,
I bottled and diapered, I cuddled and kissed.
Amazing, the know-how a grandmother learns
In the course of a lifetime and how it returns:
Three sons and three daughters and all of them grown;
indeed, I have mothered a few of my own!

The Look-Alike

I saw my mother yesterday,
across the park, and suddenly—
confused and startled—found myself
pursuing her; exhorting me,
my foolish heart. Blurred images—
how long had they been stored away?—
came in a rush, and I returned,
a child again, to yesterday.

But when I drew abreast of her
and looked into a stranger's eyes,
one image blotted out the rest:
the meadow where my mother lies.

As logic gently chided me,
my heart apologized, and then,
assured me that the day would come
when I would be with her again.

Nurse's Soliloquy

The old man dreams: what stories he could tell,
but there's no one to listen anymore,
and so behind closed eyes he wanders back
to all that he has known and loved before.
I'd listen—if I had the time to spare,
but he's just one of many in my care.

When their "demanding schedules" yield the time,
his children come to visit him, and he—
delighted—tells his tales; they stifle yawns
and wait the clock to sound and set them free.
Alone again, the old man softly sighs,
returning to the world behind his eyes.

Reaffirmation

How often I recall those two
who deeply loved, but little knew—
upon the day that they were wed—
what challenges would lie ahead;
who came to know as man and wife
the strange vicissitudes of life;
who learned that as the sun and rain
comingle, so do joy and pain.
And yet, when memory revives
the special moments of their lives—
a potpourri of smiles and tears
distributed throughout the years,
what joy, my love, it is to know
that two who wed so long ago
(if asked to make the choice again)
would choose the same as they did then.

The Old Man And The Boy

I came across them at the lake, the old man and the boy;
how poignant, their affinity; how obvious, their joy:
a lovely summer afternoon to feed the ducks and fish,
to watch the boats go sailing by, or, even, should one wish,
to search for faces in the clouds; it seemed that they would find
whatever one would choose to do the other had in mind.
I watched them till the sun went down, for I could well foresee
no pen (or brush) could recreate that golden tapestry

Ribbons

Our lives, like two bright ribbons, intertwined,
inextricably tangled, leave behind
a rich confusion; joyous colors blend.
Unfurling still, we cannot see the end
of either ribbon, but I hope that time
determines that the shorter one is mine.
If yours should prove the shorter of the two,
I won't be lost; mine leads, I know to you.

Afterword
To Jean on Our 50th Anniversary

To have found you, to have grown together, to have your friendship, to have your poetic distillation of humanity, to have your support and love and to have shared life's intertwining ribbon of experience is to have good fortune beyond anyone's dreams.

— *Gail*

December 25, 1940
December 25, 1990

Grateful acknowledgement is hereby made to the editors and publishers of the following periodicals in which many of these poems have appeared: *The Atlantic Advocate, Bride's, Country Woman, Face to Face, Faith and Inspiration, Family Life Today, Grit, Harlequin, Ideals, Lutheran Standard, Lutheran Women, Modern Maturity, N.R.T.A. Journal, Our Family,* and to *Mature Living, June 1983 - © 1983 The Sunday School Board of the Southern Baptist Convention* for *"The Recruiter".*

Additional Acknowledgements:

"Milestone" — from Home Life, Aug. 1977. © 1977 The Sunday School Board of the Southern Baptist Convention

"Femme Fatale" — from Home Life, July 1983. © 1983 The Sunday School Board of the Southern Baptist Convention

"Question: What's it Like to Rear a Large Family!" — from Home Life, Nov. 1983. © 1983 The Sunday School Board of the Southern Baptist Convention

"Seasons of a Happy Marriage" — from Home Life, Feb. 1984. © 1984 The Sunday School Board of the Southern Baptist Convention

"The Need I Have For You" — from Home Life, June 1984. © 1984 The Sunday School Board of the Southern Baptist Convention

"Summer's End" — from Home Life, Sept. 1984. © 1984. The Sunday School Board of the Southern Baptist Convention

"On Being a Parent" — from Home Life, Dec. 1984. © 1984 The Sunday School Board of the Southern Baptist Convention

"First Love" — from Home Life, June 1985. © 1985 The Sunday School Board of the Southern Baptist Convention

"Guidelines for Grandma" — from Home Life, July 1985. © 1985 The Sunday School Board of the Southern Baptist Convention